WORKBOOK

The Pro-Life Speaker Seminar
with Dr. Marc Newman

Refocus PRESS

Sevierville, Tennessee

The Pro-Life Speaker Seminar Workbook
Copyright © 2023 by Marc Newman
Published by Refocus Press, Sevierville, TN 37862
www.refocuspress.com

All rights reserved. No part of this publication may be reproduced, stored in a retrieval system, or transmitted in any form by any means, electronic, mechanical, photocopy, recording or otherwise, without the prior permission of the publisher, except for brief quotations for use in critical reviews or articles.

Cover design: Daniel O. Ojedokun
Book design: Irena Kalcheva

Printed in the United States of America

ISBN: 978-1-7351962-3-7

Table of Contents

Audience Analysis **1**
   Lesson 1 1
   Lesson 2 5

The Psychology of Attitude Change **11**
   Lesson 3 11
   Lesson 4 15

Persuasion Models **19**
   Lesson 5 19
   Lesson 6 25
   Lesson 7 29

Organization **33**
   Lesson 8 33

Delivery **41**
   Lesson 9 41
   Lesson 10 45
   Lesson 11 49

Image Management **53**
   Lesson 12 53

Fear **57**
   Lesson 13 57

Getting Your Foot in the Door **61**
   Lesson 14 61

Appendix 1: The 7-Minute Speaker Tool **69**
Appendix 2: Clear Organization Checklist **77**
Appendix 3: Speech Evaluation Tool **79**
Appendix 4: Speech Journal **95**
A Final Note From Dr. Newman **103**

Audience Analysis

Lesson 1

Introduction: "Giving a presentation" vs. "Hunting"

I. **What is an audience analysis?**

   The act of collecting information about audience members and/or organizations that will be useful in helping you to achieve your goals.

II. **What is a target audience?**

   That group, or sub-group, of individuals in attendance that you need to reach to attain your objectives.

III. Why should you analyze your target audience?

   A. Enables you to build rapport

   B. Identifies common ground

   C. Isolates potential group hot buttons

   D. Allows you to modify your presentation for maximum effectiveness

IV. Types of audiences

   A. Hostile

   B. Neutral

   C. Friendly

Lesson 1 Assignment

1. Make a list of the presentations you have delivered in the past year. List them in two columns: one column identifying the topic, and the second column identifying the group or organization you addressed. Make sure you include presentations to church boards or other small audiences.

2. Identify the attitude or leanings of each audience: hostile, neutral, or friendly, and explain why you think they fit in that category.

3. Evaluate the goals of three presentations and critically analyze whether they were a good fit for the kind of audience you addressed and the target audience you needed to reach. Explain why. If invited again, what might you do differently?

4. If your list includes few, if any, hostile groups, select two potentially hostile groups — such as a human sexuality or health class at a local secular high school or college, a liberal-leaning church, etc. Get the contact information for the person responsible for bringing in guest lecturers or speakers, and place that contact information in a file. At the end of the seminar, make contact and try to arrange speaking opportunities there.

Audience Analysis

Lesson 2

Introduction: The Pro-Life Tri-Athlete

I. **How to Analyze Your Audience**

   A. Identify the right person

   1. School:

   2. Civic Group:

   3. Church:

   B. Ask questions and take notes

II. What do we look for in an audience analysis?

   A. Common circumstances:

   1. Age, income, gender, religion, political party

   2. Isolate the factors important to the success of your message

   B. Common experiences:

   1. Are there some common occurrences that cause these particular people to meet together that transcends demographics, i.e. inequality of pay, post-abortive women?

   2. What experiences does this audience have in common that could strike a responsive chord in them if that experience was a part of your presentation?

C. Common goals:

1. What type of "world" would your audience like to see prevail? What are the factors within that vision?

2. How will your program help them toward achieving this type of "world?"

III. Gauging your topic to your audience requires an understanding of their:

A. Interest – How interested is your audience in your topic, initially? What can you do to increase their interest level?

B. Attitude – What is your audience's attitude toward your topic: favorable, neutral, or hostile? What can you do to enhance your favorability rating?

C. Knowledge — How knowledgeable is your audience about the topic? How much background is required? How much jargon will be acceptable?

Lesson 2 Assignment

1. Select a local civic group where you would like to speak, and perform an audience analysis.

   - First, research the civic group so that you have a basic knowledge of the organization's background. Pay attention to details that might be useful in your presentation.

   - Second, call or email the appropriate contact person for the group (possibly, it's the president or program planner). Identify yourself, telling them that you are interested in connecting with local leaders. Ask if they have a minute to tell you about their group. If not, ask if you can schedule a time. Tell them you want to know a little about the club to see if there is some way you can be of service.

   - Third, if they are willing to talk, ask questions that cover the three areas you want to know: circumstances, experiences, and goal. It is okay to start with a few scripted questions, but don't be afraid to ask follow-up and clarification questions. Remember, it's a conversation, not an interrogation.

   - Take notes. When the conversation winds down, thank them. Let them know that one thing your organization does is to provide speakers, and ask if they would be the right person to whom you could send a list of speakers and presentation titles that would fit the needs of the group.

   - Follow up within a week.

2. Brainstorm about how the different services you offer could extend the work of various kinds of local churches.

   - Pick at least two very different churches and look at their websites to discover what they are about, and the kinds of programs they have in place to advance their stated goals.

   - Make a thorough list of the services your organization provides.

   - For each service you listed, identify the kind of church goal it might extend (evangelism, aid to the poor, education, outreach, etc.)

Keep this list handy to help you in prepping upcoming presentations. That way you can incorporate this knowledge as part of the "goodwill" statement in your introduction, and connect it to your solution and action sections as needed.

The Psychology of Attitude Change

Lesson 3

Introduction: People are resistant to change

I. Why people are resistant to change

    A. Because they think they're right

    B. People like certainty, and want to avoid uncertainty

    C. People are ego-involved

    D. People are comfortable in their tribe

II. Two myths about attitude change

A. Magic Bullet Theory

B. Strong fear appeals
In order for fear appeals to be successful they must —

1. Come from a credible source

2. Be real to the audience

3. Be able to be handled, psychologically, by the audience

4. Have a solution that is inexpensive and easy to implement

5. Be repeated frequently

C. A word about graphic abortion images

1. Why they are important

2. Not used as a fear appeal

3. Used as support for a propositional claim

4. Useful if used correctly

III. The need for imbalance as a precursor to change

Lesson 3 Assignment

1. Identify something important about which you changed your mind, or a strong habit you eventually broke. Assuming you knew you were wrong, or that what you were doing was bad for you, why did you resist making the change?

2. The work that you do is important. The lives of unborn children are counting on it. There is the assumption that you often pray about the work of your pro-life organization. Make a pledge to pray for every remaining day of this seminar that God will make you an agent of change and that He will give you the strength, the focus, and the persistence necessary to succeed.

3. Some of the best examples of Magic Bullet Theory are New Year's Resolutions. It's a kind of single, perfect persuasive message (to yourself) designed to evoke change. Share some resolutions that failed miserably (for most people, it will be nearly all of them). What does it take to initiate real change in you?

The Psychology of Attitude Change

Lesson 4

Introduction: How we bring imbalance

I. **Defining cognitive dissonance**

   Cognitive dissonance is the psychological stress people experience when their anchor beliefs come into conflict with new information.

II. **Six strategies people use to avoid the imbalance**

   A. Selective exposure:

   B. Selective perception:

C. Selective retention:

D. Rationalize:

E. Devalue new information:

F. Devalue old information:

III. **What works?**

   A. Prolonged campaigns of persuasion: helps solve for selective exposure and selective retention

   B. Concrete word choices: helps to overcome selective perception

C. Relate to your audience: overcomes rationalization

D. Use hostile and neutral sources before biased ones: overcomes some devaluing of new information

   1. Hostile:

   2. Neutral:

   3. Biased:

Lesson 4 Assignment

1. Go back to the first part of the Lesson 3 assignment. Now you have some labels. When you were first aware that previous ideas you held to might be wrong, or that the habit you had was harmful, which of the six strategies did you employ to shield yourself from change? (You can employ more than one.)

2. How does knowing that persuasion is hard affect the way you think about your role as a persuader? How does it affect your attitude toward potentially hostile audience members?

3. Of the four strategies to overcome the difficulties presented by the way people respond to cognitive dissonance, focus on 1 and 2 (numbers 3 and 4 will be handled more extensively later in the seminar).

   - Starting with churches, strategize curriculum topics that you believe will help to create a culture of life at each developmental level: early elementary, late elementary, junior high, etc. How often can you connect with each group? If you lack the speaking staff, how can you bring more people in to handle the needed speaking assignments? How might you invite church staff and teachers to training so that they could replace you in the Sunday School and small group classes?

     Note: Once you finish the Pro-Life Speaker Seminar, arrange to meet with staff at a supportive church (at first) and talk with them about implementing a plan that will help to shield their congregation from the lure of abortion, and bring healing to those who have experienced it. Once you are well-integrated, create a strategic plan to spread this program to other churches.

   - If you have an audio or video recording of a presentation, watch it to see if you are using the language of life, or if you have been co-opted into using the language of abortion rights advocates. Have your staff evaluate their own word usage. Create accountability to shift people to language choices that affirm and uphold life.

Persuasion Models

Lesson 5

Introduction: Inoculation for disease and ideas

I. **Persuading hostile audiences or opponents: Inoculation Method**

   A. Definition: The inoculation method involves giving your audience your opponent's ideas, and then providing them with the means to fend them off.

   B. Basic Structure of Inoculation

   1. Respectfully explain your opponents' position(s)

   2. Tell your audience why your opponent's positions are flawed

3. Explain your position (if necessary)

4. Explain the impact of your argument

C. Two Methods of Approach

1. Pro-Con-Pro-Con: when time is limited

   Example
   a. Is the unborn human?
      i. They say

      ii. Their position is flawed

iii. Our position

iv. Impact

b. Is the unborn child valuable?

   i. They say

   ii. Their position is flawed

   iii. Our position

   iv. Impact

c. What about competing claims?

   i. They say

   ii. Their position is flawed

   iii. Our position

   iv. Impact

2. Set Up and Destroy: when you have more time

   a. Set up the case for abortion

b. Systematically take it apart

c. Explain your position

d. Explain the impact

Lesson 5 Assignment

1. The inoculation approach outlines the body of a presentation that you would likely use in front of a hostile or neutral audience. It really requires that you "know things." Take your time with this. The results will be useful to you throughout the rest of the Seminar and as a speaker out in the "real world."

   Brainstorm over all of the arguments you can think of that abortion rights advocates might use to justify abortion.

2. Now brainstorm possible pro-life responses to each of the arguments from the section above. If you have any pro-abortion rights arguments for which you have no good answer, mark them to be researched later.

3. Outline your position on the life issue. Think of answers from science, philosophy/ethics, and biblical sources.

4. In your own words, describe the overall impact of the total of your argumentation. If what you say is true, how should that knowledge change your audience's thinking and behavior? Be specific.

Persuasion Models

Lesson 6

Introduction: Even when people recognize the truth, how do we turn that into action? The Motivated Sequence mirrors the way people make decisions.

I. **Persuading friendly audiences: The Motivated Sequence**

   A. Get the audience's <u>Attention</u>

   B. Establish the <u>Need</u> — First point in the body

C. Explain the Solution to the problem

D. Help the audience to Visualize potential outcomes

E. Move the audience to Action

Conclusion: How will you know whether you did a good job?

Lesson 6 Assignment

1. You are going to make a presentation about your organization to either a church board or a small group Bible study — pick one. Even though this may appear to be a presentation where the key aim is to inform, it is not (and should never be).

2. Lay out a three-paragraph description of this real or fictional audience identifying their: demographics, common experiences, and common goals.

3. There are four common goals for these pro-life presentations: raise awareness of the abortion issue, or to gain prayer, volunteer, or financial support. Looking at the audience analysis, rank order these goals based on the likelihood that the identified audience would be in a position to provide what you seek.

4. Brainstorm the body of your presentation (you can skip the Attention Getting stage in this assignment — that happens in the introduction and we'll get to that later).

    You will prepare "out of order" by beginning with the Satisfaction step because everything you DO is in answer to a PROBLEM that needs to be SOLVED — and you want to keep your problem and your solution sections closely linked.

    - List and describe the goods and services your organization provides.
    - What problems are these goods and services designed to fix or manage?

    This would make up the content for your Need and Satisfaction steps.

5. People are motivated by hope of gain or fear of loss. What good outcomes could this particular audience expect to see if more people were aware of, participated in, or availed themselves of the services of your organization? What can they expect if the problem continues unabated? This will be the content for your Visualization step.

6. What specific action steps could this particular audience take to make the Satisfaction steps happen or have greater reach and impact? Remember, no generic "pray, volunteer, give" answers here. Think of the audience you've defined and outline specific actions you could ask of them. This will make up the content for your Action step. How will you follow through after your presentation?

Persuasion Models

Lesson 7

Introduction: The connection between the head and the heart

I. **Using evidence to strengthen your message**

   A. Who should use evidence?

   B. Sources of evidence:

   1. Biased:

   2. Neutral:

3. Hostile:

C. When to use evidence?

D. How to introduce evidence into your presentation:
- the name of the person you are citing
- their credentials
- the name of the publication in which the remarks appear
- the date of the publication

E. The importance of recency in statistical vs. philosophical claims

II. Emotional appeals

A. Should people use emotional appeals?

B. How to use emotional appeals ethically and effectively

III. Closing strategies

A. To help you close: Yes-yes

B. Ask Which, not If

C. Partial commitment: get some compliance and then close

Lesson 7 Assignment

1. Two key elements that constantly crop up in abortion advocacy regard the nature and value of the unborn. Think about, for example, the SLED categories. It's time to look at the abortion rights arguments you identified in the Lesson 5 assignment on inoculation, and add additional evidence and analysis to it. You will find that many of your arguments will fall in to the categories below. Research and outline what abortion rights advocates have to say about:

   - The nature of the unborn (if not human beings, what are they?)

   - The value of the unborn (since abortion rights advocates don't truly believe in the humanity of the unborn, they are assigned a different value set. Some examples might include: a burden, an inconvenience, a source of material for experimentation, etc.)

   - To whatever degree possible, cite sources to demonstrate that you haven't "made up" these claims, but that they really are advanced by abortion rights advocates

   Craft each individual argument on a separate page or on 3x5 or 4x6 cards.

2. Do research and outline pro-life responses to each of the arguments you encountered in your preparation. Clip each response to the argument it references.

3. Look at your position on the life issue you crafted in Lesson 5. Reference and cite sources for your answers from science, philosophy/ethics, and biblical sources. Note that, as your audience analysis might tell you, secular audiences might not be willing to entertain what they view as "religion-based" answers on abortion.

   NOTE: You can do this assignment individually, but if you are working as a team, each member can take on individual arguments, and then the group can come together to share resources. Make certain that everyone in the group gets a copy of each member's research. You will use them to create files that will help you to craft presentations later.

   A FURTHER NOTE ON RESEARCH: Research is never a "one and done" experience. As new articles come to light, continue to build your file.

Organization

Lesson 8

Introduction:

I. Misconceptions about presentations – or WHY I DON'T NEED TRAINING (or effort)

    A. Gift of the muses

    B. Once I begin I'll be fine

    C. "I already know how to talk"

II. Overcoming misconceptions

A. Giving presentations is a learned skill

B. Impromptu speech without training is presentation suicide

C. Conversing and speaking are two separate skills

III. Four reasons why you need to be organized:

A. Audiences need to anticipate

B. Audiences need to be able to "track" with your arguments

C. Audiences need to remember before they can act

D. Audiences need a sense of closure

IV. **Organizing**
   A. Placing ideas in conceptual boxes or "moving ideas"

   B. Avoiding leakage

   C. Breaking the speech into functions
      1. Introduction
         a. Attention getter
            i. Never say...

            ii. Audience involvement

iii. Startling statistic

iv. Tell a story

b. Introduce the topic - generally

c. Significance

d. Goodwill

e. Credibility

2. Preview of main points

3. Developing main points
   a. Narrow the content

   b. Organize the sub-points

   c. Support claims with evidence

   d. Insert internal previews if necessary

4. Transitions

5. Conclusion
   a. Wrap-up

   b. Concluding device:
      i. Delivery driven

      ii. Content driven

Lesson 8 Assignment

1. Select the basic material for either the inoculation or the motivated sequence speeches you began in the Persuasion Models section.

2. Take your material and place it into appropriate concept boxes to craft your body content. To help with this assignment, the main concept boxes are as follows:

Inoculation
   1. Arguments supporting abortion
   2. Why those arguments are wrong
   3. The position of my organization
   4. The impact of this argument

Motivated Sequence

   Note to remember: "Attention" isn't in the body of the presentation; it is the first part of the introduction.
   1. Need: what is/are the problem(s) you intend to solve?
   2. Satisfaction: what does your organization do to solve those problems?
   3. Visualization: How will engaging in the solution create a positive impact and/or how will NOT engaging in the solution create a negative outcome?
   4. Action: remember, be specific!

3. Develop your introduction for this presentation. Include all six parts of an introduction.

4. Develop each main point of the body of your presentation. Do **NOT** write out a manuscript. Use an outlining format. Try to craft a presentation you think will take 10-15 minutes to deliver.

5. Lay in your transitions between each of the main points.

6. Craft your conclusion — make sure you have both parts.

7. Make sure these are typed, not handwritten.

8. If you are working with a team, trade outlines.

9. Put on your critical glasses. Use the Clear Organization Checklist, found at the back of this workbook, to critique the structure of your outline or that of a teammate.

Delivery

Lesson 9

Introduction: What good delivery can do

I. **Eye contact**

    A. Why is eye contact important?

    B. Effective eye contact

II. **Hand gestures**

    A. How not to use your hands

        1. Fig leaf #1

        2. Fig leaf #2

3. Gunslinger

4. Superglued elbows

5. Handcuffs

6. Etch-a-sketch

7. Out of sync

8. Hand clasping

9. Spiders on a mirror

B. Gestures that work are designed to:

   1. Illustrate

   2. Punctuate

III. Facial expressions

A. Faces that create problems

B. The power of "affect display agreement"

Lesson 9 Assignment

1. Do a brief self-evaluation. Based on what you have learned so far, identify which, if any, bad delivery habits you think you have picked up. Do you have trouble making eye contact, are you a hand clasper, or inveterate smiler? Once you have identified known delivery problems, focus on making appropriate changes.

2. By now, your team should be aware of the 7-Minute Speaker Tool (explained in the appendix). You will begin working with the Current Events section. You will be sharpening your preparation and organizational skills, but you will also be actively delivering these presentations. Work with team members and live coach, and then evaluate one another. You can also practice these exercises at home. Enlist a confederate (a friend or family member). Show them what to look for in your presentation and ask them to critically evaluate your presentation.

   Use the speech evaluation form located at the back of this workbook (feel free to make extra copies of that form) to guide critiques. NOTE: Do not practice in front of a mirror. Watching yourself as you perform is too distracting.

Delivery

Lesson 10

I. Vocal delivery

   A. A question of style: Natural vs. "dynamic"

   B. Using natural skills more effectively: Vocal variety

      1. Rate

      2. Pitch

3. Volume

4. Pauses

II. Moving with purpose

    A. Common pitfalls

        1. Sea sickness

        2. Up against the wall

        3. Professional Model

        4. Expectant Father

B. When to move on the platform

    1. Transitions

    2. For emphasis

Lesson 10 Assignment

1. As in the last homework assignment, do a brief self-evaluation of your vocal variety and platform movement. Based on what you have learned so far, identify any bad delivery habits. Work with a team member to live coach you, if possible.

Delivery

Lesson 11

I. **Using Visual Aids (V.A.s) as Support in Presentations**

　A. Why use visual aids?

　　1. Problems with visual aids

　　2. Proper reasons to use visual aids

　　　a. Instant clarity for objects

　　　b. Increase understanding of complex data sets

　B. Small classroom, hand-held visual aids — Use quality presentation materials

　　1. Size

2. Lettering

3. The importance of color

C. Larger classrooms and church: Projectors, laptops, iPad pitfalls

D. Practice with visual aids before the actual presentation

E. Always cover visual aids when they are not in use

F. Never hand out visual aids during a group presentation; always after

II. Other delivery considerations

A. Using a manuscript vs. speaking extemporaneously

B. Using a microphone

   1. unidirectional

   2. omnidirectional

   3. radio

C. Using a podium or lectern

Lesson 11 Assignment

1. If your organization has used visual aids in presentations in the past, evaluate them according to the guidelines in this lesson. Which ones are useful? Which are good under some circumstances, but inappropriate in others? Which are outdated and in need of replacement?

2. What visual aids do you need to purchase or acquire? Note: At bare minimum, organizations should have intrauterine still photos and videos of developing humans. Tactile fetal models are also a must.

   Additionally, I recommend that organizations also acquire well-produced graphic abortion photos and videos. I recognize that these images are controversial, but if used properly, they can be powerful tools to break through the denial that keeps many people ignorant about the peril facing unborn children. If you choose to do so, I recommend contacting Life Training Institute to request their video "This is Abortion." It is short –about a minute – and it has no narration – it is just images and music. When using graphic images or video you must warn audiences in advance what they are about to see, let audience members know that they can choose to not look, and that you will let them know when the video is over or the images are covered. When using graphic videos, make sure that the audience is age appropriate.

3. Is your organization in need of projection equipment? If so, determine how you will acquire it.

4. If possible, bring in a lectern (a music stand will do) and a microphone on a mic stand. For a few rounds of practice, deliver your presentation, extemporaneously, from the lectern, using the microphone. Have team members evaluate your mic and lectern usage.

   If you are in the Pro-Life topics section of the 7-Minute Speaker Tool, have a variety of static visual aids (photos and models) ready and available. When appropriate, incorporate these visual aids into your presentation. (NOTE: Not all topics require the use of visual aids). Using the standards for good visual aid usage outlined in this lesson, evaluate your use. If no visual aids are called for by your topic, complete your speech assignment and evaluate as usual.

Image Management

Lesson 12

Introduction: If they don't trust you, you're done

Difference between Hollywood "image management" and image management for representatives of pro-life organizations

I. **What is "credibility?" It is the level at which you are perceived as being trustworthy and reliable**

   A. Source credibility:

   B. Derived credibility:

C. Terminal credibility:

II. **Audience perceptions of credibility**

   A. The initial impression

   1. Dress: general rule – at least one step above your audience.

      a. Men

      b. Women

NOTE: Appropriate professional attire for women changes more often than it does for men. If anything mentioned in the video is out of step with current norms, note them and discuss them after the lesson. The important point is that both men and women be attired professionally.

2. Taking the floor

3. Leaving the floor

B. Evident expertise.

1. Have your credentials established

2. Be introduced by a credible person

III. Audience granting of perceived credibility

A. Perceived preparation

B. Evident research

Lesson 12 Assignment

1. What elements of source credibility do you possess that you can leverage in the credibility section of your introduction? (Note: Don't sell yourself short!)

2. Consider past presentations you have made. Based on the material in this lesson, evaluate those presentations. Examine how you used your source credibility (if applicable), how well prepared you were, your dress, your demeanor on the platform, how well you established your credibility, your use of evidence in your arguments, etc. Identify what you did well and identify areas where you fell short. What strategies and tactics will you need to employ before your next public presentation in order to present yourself and your organization in the best possible light?

Fear

Lesson 13

Introduction: *"In time we hate that which we most often fear."* – Shakespeare

I. **The psychology of stage fright**

   A. Misconception of public speaking as a gift – and you don't have it!

   B. Fear of being judged

   C. Fear of being misunderstood

   D. Fear of humiliation

E. Fear of vulnerability

II. **The preparatory causes of stage fright**
   A. Not prepared to be a speaker

   B. Not prepared to speak today...this often leads to...

   C. The downward spiral of despair

III. **How audiences perceive your fear**

IV. **Methods of reducing fear in preparation, before, and during your presentation**
   A. Preparation

B. Before

    1. Pray

    2. Get a good night's sleep before you speak

    3. Eat light and right

    4. Walk off excess energy

    5. Run through your introduction

    6. Run through your speech structure

C. During

    1. Know that you know

    2. Remember what the audience knows

Lesson 13 Assignment

1. Write out your worst-case scenario for what might happen to you at a speaking engagement. Take your time.

2. Evaluate the likelihood of all of the elements of that scenario unfolding as you described it.

3. Write out your best-case scenario for what might happen as a result of a great presentation.

4. Assuming that you have done the work, including the practice sessions in this seminar, what is the likelihood that many aspects of your best-case scenario would happen?

5. Write out a one-page manifesto called "Why I Am a Voice for the Unborn." Post it in your office and refer to it whenever you feel fear creeping in.

6. As you practice, be aware of fear triggers. What methods of controlling anxiety do you find most helpful?

    Note: You'll notice that the more you practice, the less anxiety you will feel. Competence breeds confidence.

Getting Your Foot in the Door

Lesson 14

I. **Why they do not want to hear you**

   A. Divisive

   B. Unnecessary

   C. Controversial/Political

II. **How to get a hearing**

   A. Churches

   1. "Romancing" the secretary

2. Lunch

3. Desserts and open houses

   a. Understand the pecking order

   b. Be professional

4. Elder/Deacon boards

   a. Be a resource

   b. Gain confederates

5. Final thoughts on churches

   a. Be persistent

    b. Leverage the churches of your volunteers and staff

    c. Start small

B. Civic groups

  1. Recognize that they NEED SPEAKERS

  2. Put PROFESSIONAL packets together

  3. Send them out

  4. Follow-up call

  5. Start with non-threatening educational programs

C. Schools

   1. Be a resource

   2. Target classes

   3. Don't be put off by scheduling

   4. Leverage your work with civic groups

   5. Appeal to academic freedom and free speech

   6. "Dogging Planned Parenthood"

Lesson 14 Assignment

The following assignments can appear overwhelming to small organizations. Do not be afraid to move forward at your own pace — but do move forward. The fact is that most (all?) organizations work better when they are well staffed, fully funded, and have a powerful prayer support system. Reaching out in the following ways lays a solid foundation to move you toward those goals.

1. Get or craft a list of the churches attended by your staff and volunteers (later you can reach out to major donors to identify their churches as well).

    - Divide the list into Involved (churches with whom you have a formal relationship) and Uninvolved (churches where such a relationship is lacking). Further divide Uninvolved into Friendly and Hostile.

    - Leverage staff and volunteers to arrange for a designated representative from your organization to meet representatives of those Involved and Uninvolved Friendly churches (more on Uninvolved Hostile churches below). This doesn't have to be anything big and formal at first, and while an introduction to the pastor would be ideal, an introduction to the church secretary or other key personnel would be a great first step. Begin with Involved, then Uninvolved Friendly churches.

    - No appeals for support should be made until you have been serving that church. Start by asking questions about them, the church, how the pastor or secretary got involved there, etc. Tell them BRIEFLY about your organization and your desire to serve the area churches. Let them know about the community and educational services you provide. Ask if it would be okay to drop a packet by.

    - Try to calendar at least one of these meetings a week until you have covered every church on your list. Only then should you go out calling on other churches (and hope, by then, you can get a pastor or leader from one of your churches to make the introduction for you).

    - Follow up a week later. See if you can meet with a pastor, youth pastor, or lay leader to discuss which presentations would be most appropriate for their group. Ask them if there are other topics, not included in your packet, that they would like explored with their group. Then work to calendar a presentation. NOTE: Always bring a "speaking calendar" with you so that you avoid scheduling conflicts.

- At all presentations involving adults, pass around a clipboard asking for contact information, preferably name and email, so that you can keep them updated through your newsletter.

- After the presentation, follow up. If you spoke in a church, ask the pastor for feedback and, if it is favorable, ask if he could make an introduction to some other pastors on your organization's behalf. Emphasize your desire to be of service. If you spoke to a youth group or small group, ask if the leader could introduce you to other leaders or teachers in the church, or talk to the pastor about the quality of the presentation. See if you can arrange for other presentations at the church. If appropriate, agree to train church staff or volunteers so that they can present on these topics.

- Keep track of where you have spoken, when, and what was your topic. Create a sustainable strategy to keep speaking in that church, or to arrange to incorporate training so that appropriate topics become part of the regular curriculum for the group.

- Once you have developed a relationship with the church, pursue an opportunity to present your ministry to the congregation. Arrange ways for them to respond to a call for prayer, volunteers, and financial support.

2. Create speaker packets, customizing them for Churches, Civic Groups, and Schools.

    Packets should contain:
    - Headshots of your speakers
    - A list of sample topic titles
    - A one-paragraph description of the contents of each of those presentations
    - A one-page collection of testimonials (once you have them) from places your speakers have presented.

Note: Topics and descriptions should be carefully selected. While there will certainly be some overlap, some topics (and some content within those topics) you would present in a church may be inappropriate for a secular school or civic group. Use your audience analysis and determine which topics will be most acceptable for each group. This would also be true about testimonial pages. Have one set of testimonials for schools/civic groups, and a different one for churches. Be open to feedback and requests for alternate topics.

3. Host a pastor's dessert. Follow the format and invitation instructions outlined in this session.

Note: if you book Dr. Newman as your banquet speaker, he routinely offers pastor training lunches and/or pro-life apologetics classes as part of his itinerary. For more information, contact him through the Speaker for Life website: www.speakerforlife.com

4. Whenever a volunteer has something outstanding happen, locate the name of the volunteer's church and his or her pastor. Have someone write a thank-you letter (handwritten) to the pastor, using a variation of the general format discussed in this lesson. If you have more than one volunteer from one church, keep track so that you don't inundate the pastor with thank yous (he'll keel over). Keep a photocopy of the letters so that when you address the pastor at a later date it won't look like a form letter. After you have sent at least one thank-you letter, if a volunteer or staff member is hitting a milestone in service, contact their church and ask if you could please honor that volunteer in front of the congregation for his or her service. Keep remarks brief, 2-3 minutes, don't forget to thank the pastor, and give a tangible token of appreciation to the volunteer or staffer. People will want to know about their friend's work. Some might decide to check out your organization.

5. Once you have gotten your feet wet calendaring a few church speaking engagements, select a civic group: Lions Club, Rotary Club, or Optimist Club.

    - Contact the program planner, and ask about how far out they book their speakers.

    - Ask where you might send your speaker's packet so the planner can look over your speakers and topics.

    - Follow up in two weeks to discuss possible speaking dates. Be open to suggestions of alternate topics.

6. Finally, if you are not yet in schools, contact area public and private colleges and/or high schools.

    - Contact professors/teachers for appropriate subjects: Human Sexuality, Health, Nursing, Counseling, Women's Studies, etc. (Note: if a college, get the course schedule for the coming semester and seek out classes that might be a good fit.)

    - Explain who you are and ask about their policy regarding guest lecturers and speakers.

    - Ask where you might send your speaker's packet so the professor/teacher can look over your speakers and topics.

- Follow up in two weeks to discuss possible speaking dates. Be open to suggestions of alternate topics.

- See if the high school or college has a pro-life club or a Christian club that might invite one of your speakers to come to campus. Find out who is the contact person or sponsor, let them know what you are offering, and work out a presentation date.

- Once you have established a relationship with area junior high and high schools, consider offering an acceptable abstinence curriculum/program to the school.

The 7-Minute Speaker Tool

In committing to the Pro-Life Speaker Seminar, your goal is to build a set of skills that will enable you to make the case for the sanctity of human life, impact your church and surrounding community, and bring in the financial, volunteer, and prayer support your organization needs. To accomplish this goal, you will need a finely-honed set of skills.

Practice is the key to skills mastery. Always remember: Public speaking is a skill. In this appendix you will learn what to expect when you begin to practice, how the 7-Minute Speaker Tool works, how to do a critique session, and how to track your progress through journaling.

What to Expect When You Begin to Practice

If you were learning to play the piano, you wouldn't anticipate that you'd be playing Bach after the first week. The good news is that learning to speak in public competently is something almost anyone can do. But you will need to practice and be gracious toward yourself as you build up your skill sets.

For your first few practice sessions, expect to be bad – possibly even worse than you initially imagined. The 7-Minute Speaker Tool approach is unlike the way you likely were taught to speak in high school or college, where most students give 3-5 speeches over a single semester. In this course you will give 14 or more separate presentations. If you had a speech class in high school or college, you may have been given days or weeks to craft your presentation. Here, you will do general topic area research before you come to class, but you will prepare your entire speaking outline in 30 minutes, and then you will stand and deliver that presentation.

Most students, at the beginning, don't think they will ever be able to do it. However, thousands of people, just like you, thought the same, but then discovered that they could. Before long, you will recognize that the pressure of a short prep time, on topics about which you have knowledge, actually helps you to focus clearly on the task. In the "real world" you will rarely have to prep a speech in 30 minutes, but because you know you can – because you have proven you know how to organize a presentation – you will find your confidence growing.

You don't need to be great all at once. While you will always strive to give a complete speech, the goal for each presentation is that you pick up two skills per practice. For example, since there are only ten or so structural elements in a speech, if you picked up two per presentation, by your fifth presentation your organization should be solid. So don't be concerned about how your first few speeches turn out; focus instead on developing each skill.

How the 7-Minute Speaker Tool Works

This practice element of the Pro-Life Speaker Seminar is divided into two sections: Current Events and Pro-Life Topics. The reason we begin with current events is that many people working in pro-life organizations already think they have a clear grasp on the abortion issue. The goal is to get you out of your comfort zone in the beginning so that you can focus on structure first before content.

Research Area Preparation

To begin, your seminar leader will give you up to five research areas, drawn from current events, that you will need to research before speeches begin. Your task will be to locate, print out, and read at least 3 articles on each research area. As you read, bracket important arguments, statistics, analysis, or testimony, and write in the margins the argument each supports. Doing this will help you quickly scan an article's contents. If you find any good stories or startling statistics that would make good attention getters, note those in the margins as well. Once you have read and marked up all of your articles, it may be useful for you to place them into folders by subject to make them easier to retrieve later.

Later in class, you will move from current events to pro-life topics. As you research in this area, create careful files, since you are likely to use the contents of these files for presentations long after this class this over. When you move to pro-life topics, the slips of paper you will receive will not be questions, but scenarios that explain what kind of presentation you will have to prepare. As you advance in your preparation, you will discover that certain elements of your presentation will incorporate the same or similar content. Creating prep cards of common main points will help you to prep faster.

Getting Your Topic Question

At the start of class on speech days, you will pull out three slips of paper from your topic envelope, each with a question or scenario on it. You have two minutes to read all three slips and then select one to answer or respond to for your presentation.

Place the two slips you rejected back in the envelope – you may see them again later. Once you have selected your topic, you must prepare on that topic. Don't second-guess yourself. Trust that you chose the best one the first time.

At the end of two minutes, the class will have 30 minutes to prepare presentations. Someone in the group should keep time by calling out "fifteen minutes remaining," then ten, five, one, and finally "time's up." If no one is keeping prep time, set alarms on your phone instead.

How to Prep and Speak

Once you have settled on the question your presentation is designed to answer, begin your prep by breaking down the question into the parts that will help you to answer it. You are going to find that topic analysis is often hinted at in the question. For example, if you received the question: "Should the U.S. increase restrictions on immigration?" How might your analysis go?

Concept Boxes

Start with getting general material into your concept boxes. Here are some obvious Concept Boxes that might come from the topic "Should the U.S. increase restrictions on immigration?"

The first issue you need to consider is Why? Call your first concept box CONTEXT. You'd have to explain the context of the current immigration crisis, and perhaps identify the current restriction levels, to explain why the U.S. is even considering increasing restrictions on immigration.

The second and third Concept Boxes would be filled with arguments in favor of – and arguments opposed to – increasing restrictions. Call them PRO and CON.

For your fourth Concept Box, call it ANALYSIS. You'd need to analyze the competing claims and jot down reasons why you find one side more compelling than the other. The content of this box will aid you in answering the question.

Without muddying the waters too much, remember that there are three potential answers to that question: 1) Agree, restrictions should increase. 2) Disagree, restrictions should remain as they are, or 3) Disagree, restrictions should decrease.

Outlining the Body

Now, pull out your 3x5 or 4x6 cards – no sheets of paper. Begin with the body, and outline your first main point. It is impossible to write a manuscript for a 7-minute speech in 30 minutes – so don't even try. Usually it takes students a few tries to believe this next statement, but it is true: Write Less — Speak More. The more you try to write out your speech, the better chance you won't hit the time limits. But, if you're not tied to a manuscript and you see you are going short, you can always elaborate.

Outline your first main point from your CONTEXT concept box, using only phrases to help you remember what you want to talk about. Use proper outlining format, including indentation.

If you have source materials, paraphrase the content, but write the citation on your card. Common abbreviations can be NYT for New York Times, LAT for Los Angeles Times, WSJ for Wall Street Journal, N for Newsweek, T for Time, etc. You'll work out your own system.

First point done? Good. Repeat until the body of the speech is complete.

Next, lay in your transitions, then go back to the top and prep your introduction.

Outlining the Introduction and Conclusion

Minimally you will have 4 parts in your intro:

- attention getter
- generally state your topic verbatim (in "current events" you will read the question you will be answering, in pro-life topics you will create your own)
- create a significance statement
- a preview of main points

In this intro, you might open with a heartwarming story of newly arrived immigrants, or a horrific story of immigrant criminal activity — this is your attention getter.

Then you might say, "Stories like this one make me wonder: 'Should the U.S. increase restrictions on immigration?'" This is generally stating the topic.

For significance, maybe I found a good statistic: "Since X number of immigrants arrive or flood this country every year, it may be time to reevaluate our immigration policy."

Next, you may or may not need a goodwill statement and, unless you moonlight as a foreign policy analyst, you probably won't have a credibility statement.

Finally, you need to preview your main points. For example:

> To determine whether the U.S. should increase restrictions on immigration, I'd like to explain the current state of our immigration policy, look at arguments in favor of restrictions, and arguments opposed, and then evaluate those reasons so we can come to an informed conclusion.

Now craft the conclusion, and don't forget your wrap-up – where you reemphasize the major points of your presentation — and your concluding device.

The ultimate goal of the presentation is to answer the question. The ultimate goal of the Current Event exercise is teaching you to have all the parts of your organizational structure in place. Feel free to have your notebook open to the organization checklist so that you can check your organizational structure and make sure all the parts are there.

When you first start this prep process, you may wonder if you will *ever* prep in time. Believe it or not, once you've done this often enough, you will find you can actually prep in 15 minutes, and then quickly run through your presentation twice before delivering it in your practice group.

Stand and Deliver

When it is your turn, stand and deliver the presentation as best you can with the material you have prepared. You may be tempted to continue prepping while another person in your group is speaking. Resist that temptation. Once the speech round begins – assuming you are not the first speaker – the job of the other people in your group is to listen attentively and then critique. Give every speaker the courtesy you want extended to you.

Take the platform, make sure you have your group's attention before you begin, and then launch directly into your attention getting device. At first, don't worry much about your delivery, that will come once you can consistently speak with structure. Keep an eye on the timekeeper, and if you appear to be going short (for example, you are finishing your second main point, and the timekeeper indicates that you have four minutes left), slow down and elaborate, explain, perhaps throw in an additional example. When you are done, or if the time runs out, finish up, and then – once everyone is done – move on to the critique portion of the tool.

Evaluation

The goal of evaluation is to help everyone in the group to become more competent speakers. The first rule of group critique is that no one gets a critique until everyone has completed their speeches. When you are not speaking, have a copy of the Clear Organization Checklist evaluation sheet handy. You will find it in the back of this workbook. Your job is to listen and watch carefully, and take notes as the speech is presented.

At first, pay attention to the speaker's organizational structure. If a speaker has a very clear attention getter or has an effective wrap-up or concluding device – note that. If you notice an element that is missing — no preview of points or transitions, for example — note that omission. Once everyone's structure is solid, begin paying more attention to delivery, and then analysis.

At the completion of each round of speeches, start the round of critique with the first speaker. How you express evaluative comments – particularly improvement comments — is very important. Instead of saying something like, "Your transitions were bad!" try, instead, "I had a hard time following when you moved from one main point to another. I think the transitions need to be developed." When learning to give presentations, no one does anything "bad" or "wrong," they just have areas that "need improvement."

Each person in the group should begin by telling the speaker two things they did well. Then each person should share two things that the speaker could to do improve (and if you can give an example of how it could be improved, that is a plus). For example, maybe the speaker forgot to incorporate a transition between the first two main points. You might call that out, and add, "Transitions are supposed to review and preview, so maybe something like 'Now that you know that embryologists agree that human life begins at conception, let's look at why that matters.'"

Finally, whoever is keeping time should be able to tell the speakers the length of each presentation.

Journaling

During the practice session evaluation, you should be taking notes regarding the critique of your presentation: both the elements that were done well, and the areas you need to improve. You can also take some reflective notes of your own about how well prepared you were for that round of speeches, how you used your prep time, your own thoughts about your structure, delivery, and analysis, etc. Put all of this into a journal entry. You will find a journal area at the back of this workbook, or you can create your own on your computer if you'd prefer to take notes that way.

Each journal entry should have a date, the topic you spoke on, the length of your presentation (note whether you were under- or over-time). Then you should identify what you did well and what you need to do to improve. Finally, and this is important, select two – just two – elements where you need improvement, and commit to focus on those for your next presentation.

Journaling will help you to keep track of your progress and form a plan of improvement. You will find that as you give each new presentation – with a plan to reinforce your already solid presentation skills and add or correct just two structure, delivery, or analysis areas – you will steadily get better and better. Practice, guided by critique and reflection, will yield results.

Clear Organization Checklist

I. **Introduction: no more than 10-15% of your speech**
   - ☐ Clear attention-getting device
   - ☐ Clear statement of topic
   - ☐ Establish significance
   - ☐ Establish goodwill (if needed)
   - ☐ Establish credibility (if needed)
   - ☐ Clear preview of main points

II. **Main points**
   - ☐ Each point is a clear idea which could stand on its own
   - ☐ Substructure is clear and logical
   - ☐ All substructure addresses the main point; does not "bleed" into other points
   - ☐ Main points follow the order laid out in the preview of main points

III. **Transitions**
   - ☐ Transitions exist between each of the main points

IV. **Wrap-up**
   - ☐ Wrap-up expands on preview of main points
   - ☐ Wrap-up mirrors order of preview of main points

V. **Conclusion**
   - ☐ Conclusion reinforces overall message
   - ☐ Conclusion uses a solid concluding device
   - ☐ Final line is clearly the end; there is no need to say "thank you"

7-Minute Speaker Tool Evaluation Form

Make as many copies as you need for your organization.

Organization   **Comments**

Attention getter
States the topic
Significance
Preview of main points
Clarity of main points
Use of supporting materials
Source citation
Effective use of transitions
Clear wrap-up
Use of concluding device

General notes:

Delivery

Good eye contact
Effective vocal delivery
Effective gestures
Good platform movement

General notes:

Analysis

Speech used an appropriate format
Logical progression of ideas

For Current Events:
Provided context for the question
Hit on key components of controversy
Answered the question

For Pro-Life Topics
Audience analysis taken into account
Selected appropriate format
Selected appropriate goals
Executed the format well
Effective impact or action step

General notes:

7-Minute Speaker Tool Evaluation Form

Organization

Attention getter
States the topic
Significance
Preview of main points
Clarity of main points
Use of supporting materials
Source citation
Effective use of transitions
Clear wrap-up
Use of concluding device

General notes:

Delivery

Good eye contact
Effective vocal delivery
Effective gestures
Good platform movement

General notes:

Analysis

Speech used an appropriate format
Logical progression of ideas

For Current Events:
Provided context for the question
Hit on key components of controversy
Answered the question

For Pro-Life Topics
Audience analysis taken into account
Selected appropriate format
Selected appropriate goals
Executed the format well
Effective impact or action step

General notes:

Comments

7-Minute Speaker Tool Evaluation Form

Organization

Attention getter
States the topic
Significance
Preview of main points
Clarity of main points
Use of supporting materials
Source citation
Effective use of transitions
Clear wrap-up
Use of concluding device

General notes:

Delivery

Good eye contact
Effective vocal delivery
Effective gestures
Good platform movement

General notes:

Analysis

Speech used an appropriate format
Logical progression of ideas

For Current Events:
Provided context for the question
Hit on key components of controversy
Answered the question

For Pro-Life Topics
Audience analysis taken into account
Selected appropriate format
Selected appropriate goals
Executed the format well
Effective impact or action step

General notes:

Comments

7-Minute Speaker Tool Evaluation Form

Organization

Attention getter
States the topic
Significance
Preview of main points
Clarity of main points
Use of supporting materials
Source citation
Effective use of transitions
Clear wrap-up
Use of concluding device

General notes:

Delivery

Good eye contact
Effective vocal delivery
Effective gestures
Good platform movement

General notes:

Analysis

Speech used an appropriate format
Logical progression of ideas

For Current Events:
Provided context for the question
Hit on key components of controversy
Answered the question

For Pro-Life Topics
Audience analysis taken into account
Selected appropriate format
Selected appropriate goals
Executed the format well
Effective impact or action step

General notes:

Comments

7-Minute Speaker Tool Evaluation Form

Organization

Attention getter
States the topic
Significance
Preview of main points
Clarity of main points
Use of supporting materials
Source citation
Effective use of transitions
Clear wrap-up
Use of concluding device

General notes:

Delivery

Good eye contact
Effective vocal delivery
Effective gestures
Good platform movement

General notes:

Analysis

Speech used an appropriate format
Logical progression of ideas

For Current Events:
Provided context for the question
Hit on key components of controversy
Answered the question

For Pro-Life Topics
Audience analysis taken into account
Selected appropriate format
Selected appropriate goals
Executed the format well
Effective impact or action step

General notes:

Comments

7-Minute Speaker Tool Evaluation Form

Organization　　　　　　　　　　　　**Comments**

Attention getter
States the topic
Significance
Preview of main points
Clarity of main points
Use of supporting materials
Source citation
Effective use of transitions
Clear wrap-up
Use of concluding device

General notes:

Delivery

Good eye contact
Effective vocal delivery
Effective gestures
Good platform movement

General notes:

Analysis

Speech used an appropriate format
Logical progression of ideas

For Current Events:
Provided context for the question
Hit on key components of controversy
Answered the question

For Pro-Life Topics
Audience analysis taken into account
Selected appropriate format
Selected appropriate goals
Executed the format well
Effective impact or action step

General notes:

7-Minute Speaker Tool Evaluation Form

Organization

Attention getter
States the topic
Significance
Preview of main points
Clarity of main points
Use of supporting materials
Source citation
Effective use of transitions
Clear wrap-up
Use of concluding device

General notes:

Delivery

Good eye contact
Effective vocal delivery
Effective gestures
Good platform movement

General notes:

Analysis

Speech used an appropriate format
Logical progression of ideas

For Current Events:
Provided context for the question
Hit on key components of controversy
Answered the question

For Pro-Life Topics
Audience analysis taken into account
Selected appropriate format
Selected appropriate goals
Executed the format well
Effective impact or action step

General notes:

Comments

7-Minute Speaker Tool Evaluation Form

Organization

Attention getter
States the topic
Significance
Preview of main points
Clarity of main points
Use of supporting materials
Source citation
Effective use of transitions
Clear wrap-up
Use of concluding device

General notes:

Delivery

Good eye contact
Effective vocal delivery
Effective gestures
Good platform movement

General notes:

Analysis

Speech used an appropriate format
Logical progression of ideas

For Current Events:
Provided context for the question
Hit on key components of controversy
Answered the question

For Pro-Life Topics
Audience analysis taken into account
Selected appropriate format
Selected appropriate goals
Executed the format well
Effective impact or action step

General notes:

Comments

7-Minute Speaker Tool Evaluation Form

Organization

Attention getter
States the topic
Significance
Preview of main points
Clarity of main points
Use of supporting materials
Source citation
Effective use of transitions
Clear wrap-up
Use of concluding device

General notes:

Delivery

Good eye contact
Effective vocal delivery
Effective gestures
Good platform movement

General notes:

Analysis

Speech used an appropriate format
Logical progression of ideas

For Current Events:
Provided context for the question
Hit on key components of controversy
Answered the question

For Pro-Life Topics
Audience analysis taken into account
Selected appropriate format
Selected appropriate goals
Executed the format well
Effective impact or action step

General notes:

Comments

7-Minute Speaker Tool Evaluation Form

Organization   **Comments**

Attention getter
States the topic
Significance
Preview of main points
Clarity of main points
Use of supporting materials
Source citation
Effective use of transitions
Clear wrap-up
Use of concluding device

General notes:

Delivery

Good eye contact
Effective vocal delivery
Effective gestures
Good platform movement

General notes:

Analysis

Speech used an appropriate format
Logical progression of ideas

For Current Events:
Provided context for the question
Hit on key components of controversy
Answered the question

For Pro-Life Topics
Audience analysis taken into account
Selected appropriate format
Selected appropriate goals
Executed the format well
Effective impact or action step

General notes:

7-Minute Speaker Tool Evaluation Form

Organization   **Comments**

Attention getter
States the topic
Significance
Preview of main points
Clarity of main points
Use of supporting materials
Source citation
Effective use of transitions
Clear wrap-up
Use of concluding device

General notes:

Delivery

Good eye contact
Effective vocal delivery
Effective gestures
Good platform movement

General notes:

Analysis

Speech used an appropriate format
Logical progression of ideas

For Current Events:
Provided context for the question
Hit on key components of controversy
Answered the question

For Pro-Life Topics
Audience analysis taken into account
Selected appropriate format
Selected appropriate goals
Executed the format well
Effective impact or action step

General notes:

7-Minute Speaker Tool Evaluation Form

Organization

Attention getter
States the topic
Significance
Preview of main points
Clarity of main points
Use of supporting materials
Source citation
Effective use of transitions
Clear wrap-up
Use of concluding device

General notes:

Delivery

Good eye contact
Effective vocal delivery
Effective gestures
Good platform movement

General notes:

Analysis

Speech used an appropriate format
Logical progression of ideas

For Current Events:
Provided context for the question
Hit on key components of controversy
Answered the question

For Pro-Life Topics
Audience analysis taken into account
Selected appropriate format
Selected appropriate goals
Executed the format well
Effective impact or action step

General notes:

Comments

7-Minute Speaker Tool Evaluation Form

Organization

Attention getter
States the topic
Significance
Preview of main points
Clarity of main points
Use of supporting materials
Source citation
Effective use of transitions
Clear wrap-up
Use of concluding device

General notes:

Delivery

Good eye contact
Effective vocal delivery
Effective gestures
Good platform movement

General notes:

Analysis

Speech used an appropriate format
Logical progression of ideas

For Current Events:
Provided context for the question
Hit on key components of controversy
Answered the question

For Pro-Life Topics
Audience analysis taken into account
Selected appropriate format
Selected appropriate goals
Executed the format well
Effective impact or action step

General notes:

Comments

7-Minute Speaker Tool Evaluation Form

Organization   **Comments**

Attention getter
States the topic
Significance
Preview of main points
Clarity of main points
Use of supporting materials
Source citation
Effective use of transitions
Clear wrap-up
Use of concluding device

General notes:

Delivery

Good eye contact
Effective vocal delivery
Effective gestures
Good platform movement

General notes:

Analysis

Speech used an appropriate format
Logical progression of ideas

For Current Events:
Provided context for the question
Hit on key components of controversy
Answered the question

For Pro-Life Topics
Audience analysis taken into account
Selected appropriate format
Selected appropriate goals
Executed the format well
Effective impact or action step

General notes:

7-Minute Speaker Tool Evaluation Form

Organization

Attention getter
States the topic
Significance
Preview of main points
Clarity of main points
Use of supporting materials
Source citation
Effective use of transitions
Clear wrap-up
Use of concluding device

General notes:

Delivery

Good eye contact
Effective vocal delivery
Effective gestures
Good platform movement

General notes:

Analysis

Speech used an appropriate format
Logical progression of ideas

For Current Events:
Provided context for the question
Hit on key components of controversy
Answered the question

For Pro-Life Topics
Audience analysis taken into account
Selected appropriate format
Selected appropriate goals
Executed the format well
Effective impact or action step

General notes:

Comments

Pro-Life Speaker Seminar Journal

Speech 1

Date: .... Length of speech: ....

Topic question:
....
....

What I did well:
....
....

What I need to do to improve:
....
....
....

Two elements I will focus on for my next presentation:
....
....

Speech 2

Date: .... Length of speech: ....

Topic question:
....
....

What I did well:
....
....

What I need to do to improve:
....
....
....

Two elements I will focus on for my next presentation:
....
....

Speech 3

Date: .... Length of speech: ....

Topic question:

....

What I did well:

....
....

What I need to do to improve:

....
....

Two elements I will focus on for my next presentation:

....
....

Speech 4

Date: .... Length of speech: ....

Topic question:

....

What I did well:

....
....

What I need to do to improve:

....
....

Two elements I will focus on for my next presentation:

....
....

Speech 5

Date: .... Length of speech: ....

Topic question:

....

What I did well:

....
....
....

What I need to do to improve:

....
....
....

Two elements I will focus on for my next presentation:

....
....
....

Speech 6

Date: .... Length of speech: ....

Topic question:

....

What I did well:

....
....
....

What I need to do to improve:

....
....
....

Two elements I will focus on for my next presentation:

....
....

Speech 7

Date: .... Length of speech: ....

Topic question:

....

What I did well:

....
....

What I need to do to improve:

....
....

Two elements I will focus on for my next presentation:

....
....

Speech 8

Date: .... Length of speech: ....

Topic question:

....

What I did well:

....
....

What I need to do to improve:

....
....

Two elements I will focus on for my next presentation:

....
....

Speech 9

Date: Length of speech:

Topic question:

What I did well:

What I need to do to improve:

Two elements I will focus on for my next presentation:

Speech 10

Date: Length of speech:

Topic question:

What I did well:

What I need to do to improve:

Two elements I will focus on for my next presentation:

Speech 11

Date: .... Length of speech: ....

Topic question:

....

What I did well:

....
....

What I need to do to improve:

....
....

Two elements I will focus on for my next presentation:

....
....

Speech 12

Date: .... Length of speech: ....

Topic question:

....

What I did well:

....
....

What I need to do to improve:

....
....

Two elements I will focus on for my next presentation:

....
....

Speech 13

Date: .... Length of speech: ....

Topic question:

....

What I did well:

....
....
....

What I need to do to improve:

....
....
....

Two elements I will focus on for my next presentation:

....
....
....

Speech 14

Date: .... Length of speech: ....

Topic question:

....

What I did well:

....
....
....

What I need to do to improve:

....
....
....

Two elements I will focus on for my next presentation:

....
....

Speech 15

Date: ....   Length of speech: ....

Topic question:

....

What I did well:

....
....
....

What I need to do to improve:

....
....
....

Two elements I will focus on for my next presentation:

....
....
....

Speech 16

Date: ....   Length of speech: ....

Topic question:

....

What I did well:

....
....
....

What I need to do to improve:

....
....
....

Two elements I will focus on for my next presentation:

....
....

A Final Note From Dr. Newman

"I want to know of your progress..."

Congratulations! You have completed the Pro-Life Speaker Seminar. You've put in a lot of work, and you are a better speaker on behalf of your center, clinic or advocacy group.

Now, I'd like you to do me a favor.

Look over your journal, and then write a few paragraphs to Speaker for Life about your journey as a speaker. Explain the level of speaking confidence and competence you had when you began, the progress you have made as you worked through the seminar, and any successes you have had as a speaker during or since completing the seminar.

Please send your story to:
myspeakerstory@speakerforlife.com

I'm looking forward to hearing about your experience.

May God richly bless you as you stand in the gap, speaking for your fellow image-bearers who cannot speak for themselves.

In His Grip,
Marc Newman, Ph.D.
President
Speaker for Life

www.ingramcontent.com/pod-product-compliance
Lightning Source LLC
Chambersburg PA
CBHW081403070526
44583CB00020B/2660